All About Dinosaurs

Triceratops

Daniel Nunn

Raintree is an imprint of Capstone Global Library Limited, a company incorporated in England and Wales having its registered office at 7 Pilgrim Street, London, EC4V 6LB – Registered company number: 6695582

www.raintreepublishers.co.uk
myorders@raintreepublishers.co.uk

Text © Capstone Global Library Limited 2015
First published in paperback in 2016
The moral rights of the proprietor have been asserted.

Edited by Daniel Nunn and James Benefield
Designed by Tim Bond
Picture research by Tracy Cummins
Production by Helen McCreath
Originated by Capstone Global Library Ltd
Printed and bound in China

ISBN 978 1 4062 8087 6 (hardback)
18 17 16 15 14
10 9 8 7 6 5 4 3 2 1

ISBN 978 1 4062 8094 4 (paperback)
19 18 17 16 15
10 9 8 7 6 5 4 3 2 1

British Library Cataloguing in Publication Data
A full catalogue record for this book is available from the British Library.

Acknowledgements
We would like to thank the following for permission to reproduce photographs: Alamy pp. 4 (© Michele Burgess), 6 (© David Davis Photoproductions), 9 (© Jeff Morgan 01), 10 (© blickwinkel), 11 (© Jeff Morgan 05), 18 (© Phil Degginger), 21 (© Koichi Kamoshida/ Jana Press/ ZUMAPRESS.com), 23 (© Phil Degginger); Getty Images 19 (O. Louis Mazzatenta), 20 (Maria Stenzel); Photoshot p. 12 (Jane Burton); Science Source pp. 8 (Roger Harris), 15 (Christian Dark), 17 (Mauricio Anton); Shutterstock pp. 5a (Elenarts), 5b (Matt Jeppson), 5c (Oleg Lopatkin), 5d (kajornyot), 7 left (leonello calvetti), 7 right (Michael Shake), 7 scale (Pixel-3D), 16 (Creative Travel Projects), 23 (kajornyot); Superstock pp. 13, 14 (Stocktrek Images).

Cover photograph of a ten tonne Triceratops in a Cretaceous forest in what is today the western United States, reproduced with permission of Superstock (Stocktrek Images).

Back cover photo of Triceratops reproduced with permission of Shutterstock (Elenarts).

We would like to thank Dee Reid and Nancy Harris for their invaluable help in the preparation of this book.

Every effort has been made to contact copyright holders of material reproduced in this book. Any omissions will be rectified in subsequent printings if notice is given to the publisher.

Contents

Meet Triceratops

Triceratops was a dinosaur.

Dinosaurs lived long ago.

dinosaur

snake

crocodile

lizard

Dinosaurs were reptiles.
Snakes, crocodiles and lizards
are reptiles that live today.

What was Triceratops like?

Triceratops was a big and heavy dinosaur.

Triceratops was as heavy as three cars!

Triceratops had strong and wide legs.

Triceratops had a huge head.

frill

Triceratops had a frill around its neck.

horns

Triceratops had three horns.

Triceratops ate plants.

Other dinosaurs tried to eat
Triceratops.

Triceratops used its horns to
fight back.

Triceratops lived with other Triceratops.

Where is Triceratops now?

Triceratops is extinct. There are no
Triceratops alive now.

All the dinosaurs died long ago.

fossil

We learn about Triceratops
from fossils.

Fossils are animal bones that have turned to rock.

People find fossils in the ground.

Fossils show us what Triceratops looked like.

Where in the world?

Triceratops fossils have been found in the United States and Canada.

Picture glossary

 **fossil** animal bones or parts of a plant that have turned into rock

 **reptile** cold-blooded animal. A lizard is a reptile.

How to say it

Triceratops: say 'try-sair-uh-tops'

Index

Notes for parents and teachers

Before reading

Ask the children to name some dinosaurs. Ask them if dinosaurs are around today. Talk about how some dinosaurs ate plants and others ate other dinosaurs. Can they think of ways these dinosaurs might have been different? Have they heard of Triceratops? Find out if they already know anything about this dinosaur.

After reading

- Talk about Triceratops's name. Can the children think of any other words that begin with 'tri-'? What do things like a tricycle and a triangle have in common? How many horns did Triceratops have? Why did it need these horns? Ask the children if they can think of any animals living today that use horns like this to protect themselves.
- Ask the children to make a Triceratops using junk modelling. Talk about how they might make the horns on the dinosaur's head. Will it have long or short legs?